The *Psionic Generator*
PATTERN BOOK

The PSIO

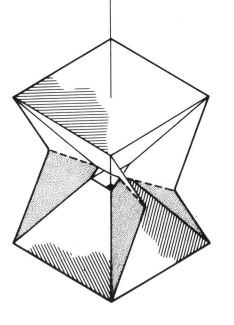

NIC

Generator
PATTERN
BOOK

by JOHN P. BOYLE

PRENTICE-HALL, INC., *Englewood Cliffs, New Jersey*

Acknowledgments

The author is deeply grateful to Sheila Ostrander, Lynn Schroeder, Woodrow W. Ward, and George L. Brandes for allowing reference to their works. Their assistance has provided a constant source of inspiration.

The Psionic Generator Pattern Book by John P. Boyle
Copyright © 1975 by John P. Boyle
All rights reserved. No part of this book may be reproduced in any form or by any means, except for the inclusion of brief quotations in a review, without permission in writing from the publisher.
Printed in the United States of America
Prentice-Hall International, Inc., London
Prentice-Hall of Australia, Pty. Ltd., Sydney
Prentice-Hall of Canada, Ltd., Toronto
Prentice-Hall of India Private Ltd., New Delhi
Prentice-Hall of Japan, Inc., Tokyo

10 9 8 7 6 5 4 3 2

Library of Congress Cataloging in Publication Data
Boyle, John P
  The psionic generator pattern book.
  1. Occult sciences. I. Title.
BF1999.B654   133'.028   74-34292
ISBN 0-13-736975-1

Contents

I. *Basic Six-Inch Pyramid*

Patterns, pages 27-35

In 1970 Sheila Ostrander and Lynn Schroeder's *Psychic Discoveries Behind the Iron Curtain* revealed that a precisely constructed pyramid shape will sharpen dull razor blades and dehydrate organic matter.

The book's editor decided to test this for himself. He bought two slices of Muenster cheese from the Prentice-Hall cafeteria and arranged one inside a makeshift cardboard pyramid, the other inside his desk drawer. Within a couple of days, the cheese in his desk was darkening and emitting a vile, rancid odor and had to be discarded. *Six weeks* later, the cheese inside the pyramid was still fresh-looking, but hard as plastic to the touch and extremely brittle. It had "wept" a copious amount of butterfat, but, significantly, this clear liquid was odorless and had no appearance of rancidity whatsoever.

Discovery of the pyramid effect is credited to Antoine Bovis, a Frenchman, while exploring the Great Pyramid of Cheops near Cairo. Although the pyramids of ancient civilizations exist in many parts of the world, the Great Pyramid is the most famous. Situated in the valley of the Nile at the edge of the Libyan Desert, it is not only the largest pyramid ever constructed, but the largest man-made structure on Earth! Its ninety million cubic feet are estimated to contain over 2,300,000 blocks of stone, each weighing from two up to almost sixty tons. Originally, all four sides were covered with casing stones which reflected the rays of the sun. But these were removed or destroyed by vandals after A.D. 822 when the interior of the Pyramid was penetrated by thieves in search of gold and treasure. Its base covers over thirteen acres of land and measures nearly two-thirds of a mile around the four sides. Archaeologists, engineers, and scholars are completely amazed at the precision with which the huge stones were joined together; in many areas, the seams are almost invisible. In his tour of the Pyramid, Monsieur Bovis came upon the so-called King's Chamber, constructed at a level of exactly one-third of the structure's full height. (It has been surmised that the pyramids were constructed as tombs for ruling kings, but apparently King Cheops was never buried inside his.) Bovis noticed trash cans containing the bodies of cats and other small animals that had wandered into the Pyramid's vastness, gotten lost, and died. Bovis was surprised that he could detect no smell of decay or putrefaction. His closer investigation revealed that the creatures were completely dehydrated or mummified!

Later Bovis began experimenting with small pyramid models built to the exact scale of the Great Pyramid, and proved that organic matter placed at the one-third level within the pyramid structure would dehydrate, not decay. Bovis observed that some unknown force within the pyramid stopped bacterial action and wondered if the shape of the large pyramids alone preserved any mummies buried within.

News of Bovis's research came to the attention of Karel Drbal, a Czechoslovakian radio engineer. His own experiments led to his discovery that a dull razor blade, placed at the one-third level of a small pyramid would regain its sharpness in a week's time and remain sharp if placed inside the pyramid between shaves.

All of the ancient pyramids were constructed so that each side faced one of the four cardinal points. The entrance, always on the north side, faced the North Star. Drbal had oriented his experimental models just like the ancient Egyptian pyramids, so that each one of the four sides faced a different direction; either north, south, east or west. He found that the shaving edges of a dull blade must face east and west, or the blade will not renew its sharpness. At first, Mr. Drbal found that he could shave over fifty times with one blade, and that as many as two hundred shaves could be acquired from one blue. blade. He theorized that the unknown energy accumulating inside the pyramid shape caused the metal crystals in the blade to return to their original form.

In 1959, after thoroughly testing Drbal's claim, the Czechoslovakian Patent Bureau awarded him patent number 91304 on his Cheops Pyramid Razor-Blade Sharpener. Miniature cardboard and styrofoam pyramids flooded the Czech market, and many other companies are selling cardboard and plastic experimental pyramid models in the United States today.

Experimenters have discovered that small amounts of meat, fish, eggs, or similar organic matter will not decay when placed within the pyramid at the proper one-third height. Researchers attest to the razor blade sharpening effect, but many claim that at least two weeks is required to enhance the blade's sharpness. Once sharp, however, it can be used every day if placed within the pyramid structure between shaves.

Some report varying degrees of success in purifying and improving the taste of water. A glass of cloudy, "assassinated" tap water becomes sparkling clear when placed under the pyramid for a short length of time. The taste is greatly improved, free from chlorine odors and harsh mineral effects. Water treated with pyramid energy has also been reported to improve or stimulate the growth of seeds and plants when poured over them daily; and placing a Basic Six-Inch* Pyramid over seedlings enhances their growth and eventually produces more abundant yields.

After pyramid treatment, many basic foods also manifest a definite improvement in taste: Bitterness is removed from tart fruits, harsh liquors become mellow to the taste, and the quality of tobacco is improved. Foods in pyramid-shaped containers remain fresh for a

*That is, the height of the completed pyramid from the apex to the center of the base.

greater length of time, and such packaging is now employed in some foreign countries. Many individuals state that a six-inch pyramid structure alleviates and sometimes completely anesthetizes the pain of chronic ailments. They claim no cure, however, and say simply that pain disappears when the affected area is covered with a pyramid structure. But many results indicate that pyramid energy increases mental telepathy, extrasensory perception, and related phenomena associated with the mind. In some respects, the pyramid shape seems to be a link between the individual and the Universal Mind that holds all knowledge of the past and future.

It takes just a few minutes to cut out and assemble the pre-printed triangles (Figures I-A through I-E) to form a Basic Six-Inch Pyramid for experimentation.

Assembly Instructions

1. Cut out the four triangles, Figures I-A through I-D. Working on a flat surface, join the triangles together as illustrated in Figure I-1. Tape the sides together with ¾-inch wide adhesive tape. Fold the triangles to form the pyramid and glue or tape Tab A on the inside of Edge A.
2. Assemble the two-inch base (Figure I-E), according to instructions.
3. Place a dull razor blade on the two-inch platform directly beneath the pyramid's apex (see Figure I-2). The pyramid must be oriented so that one side faces magnetic north. (Although researchers claim better results when using true north, either orientation will produce results.) The shaving edges of the blade must face east and west.

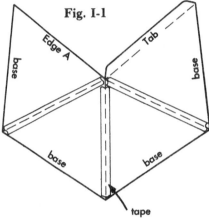

Fig. I-1

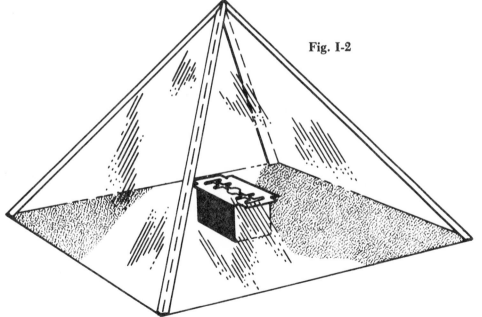

Fig. I-2

To place the pyramid and objects within precisely on a north-south/east-west orientation, use a large sheet of paper or cardboard exactly twelve inches square. Place your pyramid in the center and trace a line around the pyramid's base on the twelve-inch square. Remove the pyramid, and with a ruler, draw two diagonals on the square thus formed. When you place the pyramid on the square baseline again, the point where the diagonals cross will be directly beneath the apex.

Using a magnetic compass, you can now adjust the twelve-inch base so that the lines are oriented properly. This method assures that objects inside the pyramid are positioned accurately. Allow the blade to remain in this position for a week or longer to regain sharpness. Dehydrate organic matter in similar fashion.

When constructing larger pyramids, you must be sure the proportions are the same, and that the sides slope at the 52° angle necessary for maximum vortex energy. The crucial rule is that the total perimeter of the base divided by twice the height of the pyramid should equal pi (3.1416) or as close to it as possible. Pi divided by 2 is 1.5708. Now you can multiply this primary figure times any desired pyramid height to get the dimension for the base of one side. For instance, to find the base dimension for a six-inch pyramid, multiply 1.5708 times 6 inches. The result is 9.4248. Converting decimals into fractions gives 9-27/64 inches, for a proper base.

To find the dimensions for the equilateral sides for any given height, the rule is that the sides are 4.85% shorter than the base. 1.5708 times .04855 is .0762(62340). Subtracting .0762 from 1.5708 equals 1.4946. So you can multiply 1.4946 times any desired height to find the proper side dimensions. To continue the Basic Six-Inch Pyramid example, 1.4946 times 6 inches is 8.9676 inches, or 8-31/32 inches.

Using these formulas, the dimensions for a four-foot pyramid are: Base 75.3984 (75-25/64) inches; Sides 71.7408 (71-47/64) inches. For a three-and-a-half-foot pyramid: Base 65.9736 (65-31/32) inches; Sides 62.7732 (62-49/64) inches. And so forth.

II. *Occult Illuminator*

Patterns, pages 37-43

On September 18, 1973, United States Patent number 3,759,607 was awarded to an instrument technically called an "Occult Illuminator System," but now commonly known as the Mys-

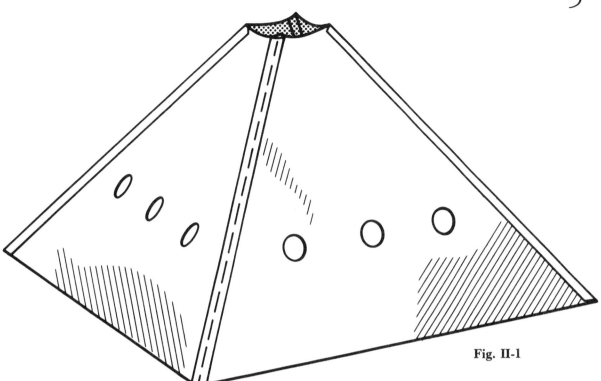

Fig. II-1

tic Pyramid. The strange effects produced by this device were stumbled on quite by accident while I was trying to develop a camera that would record photographs of thought patterns.

This device is obviously quite similar to the regular pyramid, except that the apex is cut away, providing a view of the inside. Light is also allowed to enter the pyramid's interior through small openings cut into the sides at the one-third level and is reflected from the foil-covered interior walls and mirrored base.

When one gazes into this structure for a short length of time, distinct images of beasts, human beings, and inanimate objects begin to appear, seemingly on the interior walls, in an enigmatic parade. Mathematician George L. Brandes states: "I tried the Mystic Pyramid with great success. A few minutes of gazing into the structure and visual images would burst forth into existence at random: images equal to humanoid forms, human forms, animal forms, strange structures, 'eyes' of sorts, etc. I predict that the Mystic Pyramid will set new forces in motion around the world in fields of PSI research, akin to Oersted's simple experiment in 1819 which related electricity and magnetism into electromagnetism."

As the eye travels to various areas of the pyramid, additional images will appear at random. Plugging translucent multicolored plastic fiber optics into the apertures on the sides will splash the interior of the pyramid with a spectrum of colors, bathing the images in lifelike color tones. Gold and orange optics create flesh-colored tones, while red, purple, green, and blue optics greatly enhance the enigmatic effects. Many have advanced that the basic pyramid shape scrambles or distorts time-flow patterns, producing images from the past or future. Perhaps the viewer actually sees himself in years to come or glimpses scenes from the historical past.

The Monarch Manufacturing Company (P.O. Box 187, Roseville, Michigan 48066) has been licensed to manufacture and sell the official Mystic Pyramid, constructed of high-impact styrene plastic and featuring multicolored plastic fiber optics and a mirrored base, for $20 postpaid in U.S. However, a Mystic Pyramid constructed from the patterns at the back of the book will produce many of the effects attributed to the deluxe plastic model. Although the interior will not be bathed in color, images should appear after a few minutes of gazing.

Assembly Instructions

1. Cut out the four triangles, Figures II-A through II-D. Cut out the three circular openings marked X in each triangle. Tape the triangles together at the sides, as shown in Figure II-2.
2. Place a sheet of aluminum foil over the triangles. Run your finger around the triangles' outer edges, so that their exact outline is transferred to the foil. Cut out the aluminum foil following this impressed outline.

Fig. II-2

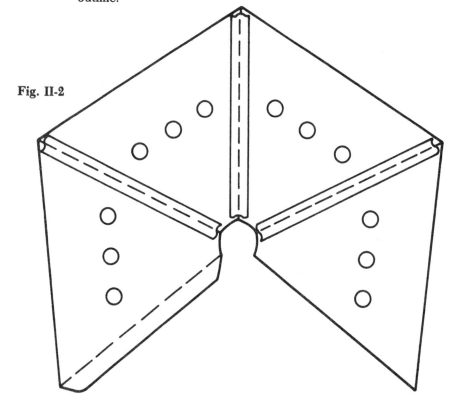

3. It's important that the foil be slightly crinkled in order to produce proper effects. Before gluing it to the triangles, simply crush the foil slightly with your hands, then smooth it out again. The necessary crinkles will remain embedded in the thin metal. Spread a light coat of glue or rubber cement on the inside ("blind") surfaces of the triangles, including the tab. Attach the aluminum foil to the triangles, *with the shiny side up*. Cut or punch out the circular openings in the foil.
4. Following the procedure for the Basic Six-Inch Pyramid, fold the four triangles to form a truncated pyramid, making sure the aluminum foil winds up inside. Glue or tape tab in place.
5. Tape a sheet of aluminum foil, shiny side up, to the base in order to reflect the interior walls. Placing the structure over a flat mirror, however, will provide even greater reflection. Make sure that the circular apertures are not blocked by foil, so that light can enter from the sides.

Visualization Method

Various degrees of lighting create different effects, but best results are achieved when the Pyramid's interior is dimly lighted. As with crystal-ball gazing, a quiet, unhurried atmosphere is most conducive.

Close one eye and place the other over the apex. Allow your eye to travel to different areas, focusing at length on the patches of light—the interior walls as reflected in the base. Moving the Pyramid or turning it to various angles changes the effect and improves results.

Many report seeing images almost immediately, while others require a week or more of regular gazing. Some experimenters state that the eye becomes tired after gazing at great length, so I recommend that you take a rest periodically.

To enhance the function of this pattern-made Pyramid, the Monarch Manufacturing Company also sells a kit containing twenty plastic fiber optics of various colors (which can be inserted in the circular openings), plus a plastic mirror for the base, for $5 postpaid in U.S.

III. *Psionic Cone Generator*

Patterns, pages 45-47

Unknown biological energies emanate from living cells. Using a method similar to Kirlian photography, scientists have actually photographed this bioenergy streaming from the human eyes. Researchers have discovered that almost all humans possess the ability to move objects at a distance through visual energy.

As early as 1921, a British doctor named Charles Russ demonstrated an apparatus which could cause a solenoid to move by gazing at it. About the same time in France, Dr. Paul Joire designed a special device with a needle that turned when a human stared at or stood near it. In recent years, Czechoslovakian Robert Pavlita has constructed generators which revolve when energy from the eyes is focused upon them.

Little is known of the Pavlita devices beyond what Ostrander and Schroeder reported in *Psychic Discoveries Behind the Iron Curtain*: They are small metal and wooden objects of various shapes and sizes which collect and store energy emanating from the human body. The secret of the generators is in their form and the juxtaposition of materials which make up the design. Combinations of copper, iron, gold, steel, and even wood are used to construct the instruments, and various shapes and sizes are used in different applications of the energy. Many of these bioenergy accumulators are etched with various designs, but more than visual energy is necessary for their operation. Holding the generator in the hands while moving the eyes along the patterns etched in the device will help it accumulate the experimenter's biological energies.

Once the Pavlita generators are charged in this fashion, they can be induced to release their energy toward other devices designed to pick it up and use it to function. A generator is pointed at a device with etchings similar to those sketched on the generator, and rests upon a spindle so that it is free to revolve. Staring at this device and following the etched patterns with the eyes will induce the instrument to activate and begin rotating.

Such biological generators are not quite so mysterious when you consider that in modern radar installations electromagnetic waves are manipulated and controlled through the use of geometric devices called wave guides. Through the use of the proper wave guide, microwave energy will follow the appropriate paths and patterns —around corners, along spiral paths, or radiated in desired configurations—to produce controlled results. The wave-guide designs do include pyramidal shapes, rectangles, spheres, and hollow tubes. Lenses of various types and sizes are used to focus microwave energy. A process called "stepping" is employed primarily to reduce weight and thickness in the lens, but any step design will tend to pick up one given wavelength, working well for that particular wavelength only. This makes the stepped lens doubly convenient, since most microwave systems center on a given radio frequency or wavelength. The Basic Six-Inch Pyramid shows that cosmic energy can be accumulated in geometric storage devices. Perhaps the ancient step pyramids found in many parts of the world were designed to pick up one particular wavelength of pyramid energy, and the ancient pyramids in various parts of the world were constructed as accumulators of cosmic energy. Also, it may well be that the Easter Island statues were built as accumulators of biological energies for an unknown purpose.

Indeed, some of the Czech generators also resemble the huge monoliths on Easter Island. In the United States, Mr. Woodrow W. Ward of Houston, Texas, took up this field of research and in 1970 invented his first generator activated by visual energy. He has since developed many similar geometric devices designed to pick up energy emanating from the eyes. According to individuals who have seen the Pavlita generators in operation, Mr. Ward's devices compare remarkably well with those of the Czech inventor.

Although similarities exist between the Pavlita and the psionic generators, there is a marked difference in basic operations. The Czech instruments first store biological energies in an inanimate object, then transfer them to the revolving device by the experimenter's staring at the patterns etched in both the generator (the "accumulator") and the revolving instrument atop the spindle. Psionic generators are activated directly from the energy streaming from the eyes.

Inspiration received from Mr. Ward's basic experiments, the study of ancient hieroglyphics, and experiments with pyramidal and conical shapes have enabled me to develop additional psionic generators. The patterns for these devices are accurate and designed for easy construction. Merely cut out the structures with scissors and fold on the broken lines, according to the instructions. (Generators constructed from paper respond more quickly than those constructed of cardboard.) A small amount of glue or cellophane tape will hold the tabs firmly in place. Quick-drying contact cement is best for rapid assembly.

Suspend the completed generator with a length of thread in a room free from air currents so that it rests at a nearly eye level position. The generator will revolve freely at first, just like any suspended object, and will take about five minutes to come to a complete stop. Then stand from five to ten feet away and concentrate your gaze upon the device. There is no need for intense concentration or projecting your thoughts. Keeping mind and body relaxed and passive is enough.

In less than a minute, the device should begin to rotate, very slowly at first. But as the energy from the eyes continues, it will begin to move faster. Shifting your gaze away from the generator, then swiftly back again seems to activate it more effectively.

Planetary configurations and especially phases of the moon tend to affect the psionic generators' response. They respond swiftly to visual bioenergy during periods of the full moon, but various times of day also find the generators extremely responsive. The earth's electrical field changes twice a day, and researchers postulate that changes in human biological energies also occur at these times. During the morning hours when the body is rested and filled with energy, the generators are activated quickly and revolve at a greater speed. When the body is fatigued, a longer period of time is required. Children, with all their unlimited energy, achieve an especially swift response when they fix their gaze upon the generators.

A glass shield placed around the devices will not prevent them from rotating. Visual energy will penetrate glass and can be reflected from mirrors, so turning your back to the generator and gazing at it through a hand mirror held in front of you will activate it.

A hundred years from now, civilization may look upon these investigations as somewhat primitive, analogous to Benjamin Franklin's electrical experiments with kite and key. When asked, "Of what use is this type of knowledge?" Franklin replied, "Of what use is a child? He may grow into a man." Although these generators exhibit little practical engineering value, it is logical to assume that many other uses remain to be discovered, once procedures for increasing the energy are worked out. Mr. Ward has also invented geometric devices which seem to accumulate and store for short periods of time biological energies emanating from the human body, and his current research is aimed at perfecting psionic devices for levitating matter and "power structures" capable of operating on nothing more than the energy accumulated within the device, providing free energy to mankind.

Certainly an unknown link seems to exist between microscopic living cell structures and their macroscopic geometric counterparts. X rays, as well as the phase-contrast and electron microscopes, reveal that many cells of the human body are geometric in structure. Brain cells may be pyramidal with one long dendrite or star-shaped with many dendrites extending in various directions. In the eye, cells differentiating between light and dark are cylindrical; those containing pigments for color vision are cone-shaped. Skeletal muscles are composed of cylindrical or prismatic fibers; red blood cells are biconcave as they mature.

Motor impulses from one side of the brain to skeletal muscles on the opposite side of the body are conducted via the pyramidal tracts, which come together and decussate in the medulla to form pyramids; hence their name. This area lies at the base of the brain near the upper portion of the neck. The larger pyramidal cells of Betz exist in the brain's primary motor region. Perhaps these microscopic pyramidal brain cells act in ways similar to the larger pyramid structures; if so, further study of brain cell structure could lead to technology on hardware levels which will make telepathic communication one hundred percent effective.

In one of his readings of future events, the great American psychic Edgar Cayce described a great crystal of precise geometric shape that would harness solar energy to levitate matter, provide new forms of communication, and regenerate and heal the human body. His prophecies spoke of tuning a crystal of this type to various degrees and pitches, performing superhuman tasks by controlling the energy concentrated within the structure. Perhaps the psionic structures —and related experimental research today—are a small step toward the day when pyramid and biological energies will be harnessed through the use of geometric shapes and forms similar to those employed in modern-day wave-guide systems.

Cytology (the study of human cell structure) and crystallography should reveal similarities and relationships between human biological systems and inanimate microscopic crystalline substances—perhaps laying down the basic laws of psionic energies and enabling us to build structures in which bioenergies can be stored and released at will through telekinesis, resulting in psionic "work force"—and perhaps developing the hardware which will lead us to the stars!

But certainly after exploring the basic fundamentals of crystallography and cytology, the ingenious experimenter will be able to create his own psionic generators, perhaps providing the controls for harnessing psionic energies. For further investigation, I would recommend *An Introduction to Crystallography* by F. C. Phillips, M.A., Ph. D. (John Wiley & Sons, Inc.), containing 534 diagrams; and *The Cell* by Carl P. Swanson (Prentice-Hall, Inc.), providing basic information on and diagrams of cell structure.

This (Figure III-1) is one of the easiest generators to construct and, although it does not revolve swiftly, is activated almost instantly when one gazes or stares at the apparatus. It is also extremely responsive to the bioenergies emanating from the human body. You can test this by placing both hands, palms up, about an inch below the bottom of the lowest cone. Both cones will vibrate slightly and begin to turn.

Assembly Instructions

1. Cut out Figures III-A and III-B and assemble the two cones.
2. Thread a needle with approximately 1½ feet of thread and tie a heavy knot at the end. Push the needle through the thread hole mark of either cone and draw the thread through until the knot catches.
3. Tie another heavy knot two inches above the apex of the cone and thread the second cone so that it rests on the second knot, about two inches above the bottom cone.
4. Suspend the cones at eye level and test the response. Since the thread holes are not at the apex, the cones will be angled at about 20°. This angle creates greater sensitivity.

Various angles create better response. You can experiment by re-threading the cones so that they rest at a greater or lesser incline.

Fig. III-1

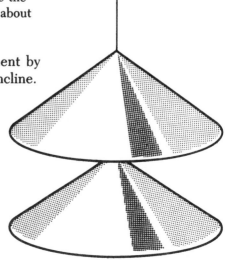

IV. *Pyramidal Generator*

Patterns, pages 49-53

Assembly Instructions

1. Cut out Figures IV-A and IV-B. Cut out the triangular openings marked X. Crease forward slightly along all broken lines and glue tabs in place to form two separate pyramidal structures.
2. Insert needle and thread with heavy knot in the end up through the apex of Structure A. Draw thread through until the knot catches and holds.
3. Tie a heavy knot in the thread approximately ¾ inch above the apex of Structure A.
4. Cut out base Figure IV-C and glue or tape tabs to the inside edge of Structure A, so that it forms a bottom.
5. Insert needle and thread through inside apex of Structure B and draw thread through until it rests on the knot approximately ¾ inch above Structure A.

Suspend the structures at approximately eye level and gaze at either structure to activate.

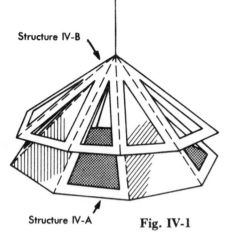

Structure IV-B

Structure IV-A   **Fig. IV-1**

V. *Cone Spire Generator*

Patterns, pages 55-61

Assembly Instructions

1. Cut out Figures V-A through V-D. Assemble the six-sided pyramidal structure (Figures V-C and V-D) and Cones V-A (Figure V-A) and V-B (Figure V-B).
2. Thread a needle and tie a heavy knot at the end. Run the needle and thread up through the apex of Cone V-B and continue through the inside apex of Cone V-A.
3. Allow Cone V-A to rest atop Cone V-B and tape in place at the base of Cone V-A.
4. Tie a heavy knot in the thread approximately two inches above the apex of Cone V-A.
5. Run the needle and thread up through the inside apex of the six-sided pyramidal structure. It should rest on the second heavy knot, allowing the bottom cones to revolve freely.
6. Suspend the generator approximately one foot above eye level and let it come to rest. Stand about eight feet away and stare at the device. If it does not begin to rotate within a minute, move to within four feet and gaze at the inside of the bottom cone. Either the cones or the pyramidal structure will revolve.

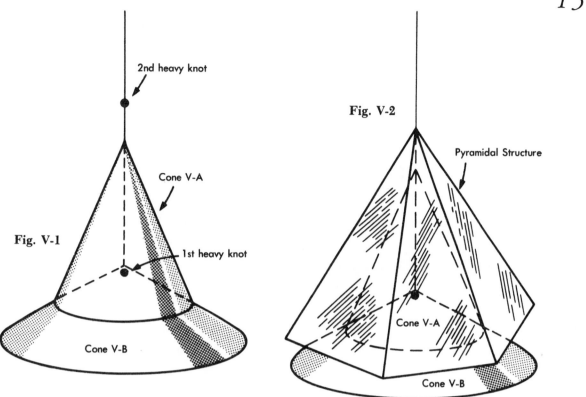

2nd heavy knot

Cone V-A

Fig. V-1

1st heavy knot

Cone V-B

Fig. V-2

Pyramidal Structure

Cone V-A

Cone V-B

Try various distances for effects but in an area free from small air currents. When moving, proceed slowly so that no air current is stirred up. Stand beneath the generator and allow an associate to observe the device as it picks up bioenergies from your body.

VI. *Conical Array Generator*

Patterns, pages 63-67

Assembly Instructions

1. Cut out and assemble Figures VI-A through VI-D, making four cones. Follow instructions for previous cone assembly, using glue or tape to secure tabs.
2. Spread glue around the bottom edge of Cone VI-B and glue this cone to the inside of Cone VI-A (see Figure VI-2).
3. Spread glue on the bottom edges of Cones VI-C and VI-D and glue one cone to the apex of Cone VI-A. Glue the remaining cone to the apex of Cone VI-B.
4. Insert needle and thread through the designated mark on Cone VI-A and suspend the structure at eye level. Gaze at the entire structure to activate.

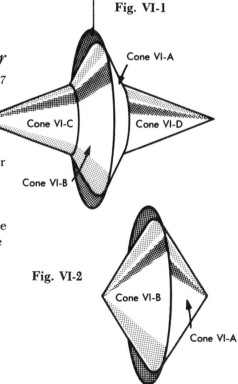

Fig. VI-1

Cone VI-A

Cone VI-C

Cone VI-D

Cone VI-B

Fig. VI-2

Cone VI-B

Cone VI-A

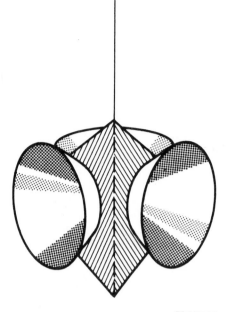

Fig. VII-1

VII. *Tetrahedron Generator*

Patterns, pages 69-73

Assembly Instructions

1. Cut out tetrahedronal pattern (Figure VII-A) along solid lines. Cut out circles marked X in each triangle. Crease along broken lines and glue or tape tab inside to form tetrahedron.
2. Cut out the three cones (Figures VII-B, VII-C, and VII-D) and follow previous cone assembly instructions.
3. Spread glue on inside edge of circular openings on the tetrahedron. Insert a cone in each opening with the apex pointing inward. Allow glue to dry, securing cones in place.
4. Thread a needle and tie a heavy knot at the end of the thread. Insert needle up through inside apex of tetrahedron and pull thread through until knot catches. Suspend at approximately eye level. Gaze at the cones to activate.

VIII. *Cone Cluster Generator*

Patterns, pages 75-77

Six cones are needed to form one Cone Cluster Generator. Twelve cones can be formed from the pre-printed patterns, so you can build two units.

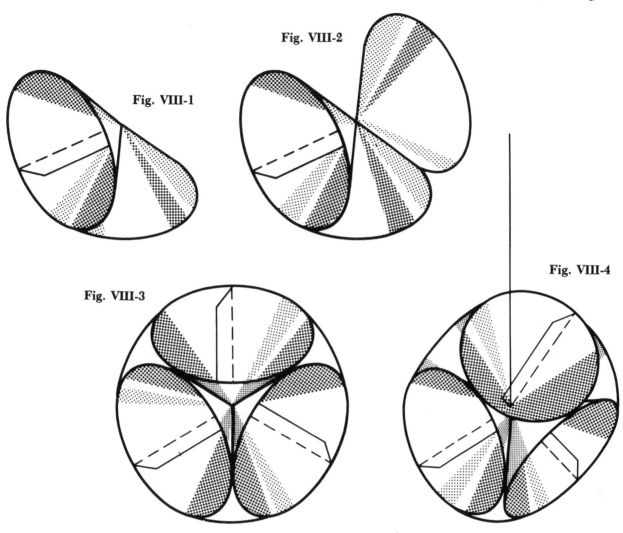

Fig. VIII-2

Fig. VIII-1

Fig. VIII-3

Fig. VIII-4

Assembly Instructions

1. Cut out Figures VIII-A through VIII-L and tape or glue the tabs inside to form the cones.
2. Use one cone for a base. Tape four cones to each side of the base cone horizontally, as shown in Figures VIII-1 and VIII-2.
3. Invert the remaining cone and tape in place as illustrated in Figure VIII-3.
4. Insert needle with knotted thread through the apex of the base cone and slightly away from the apex of the inverted cone so that the device is suspended at an angle (see Figure VIII-4).

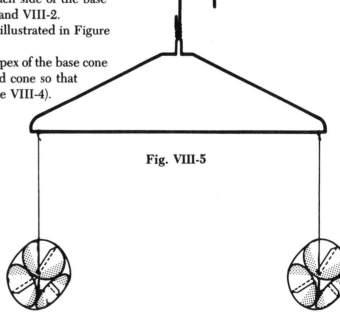

Fig. VIII-5

When activated by visual energy, this device turns a half-turn in one direction, then moves a half-turn in the opposite direction. You can demonstrate the biological energies emanating from the human body by setting up the following experiments:

Construct two Cone Cluster Generators. With sewing thread, tie one cluster to each corner of a metal coat hanger (see Figure VIII-5). Suspend the hanger at approximately eye level. When the entire apparatus is motionless, place your hands about an inch below each generator, palms up. Moving your hands in a circular pattern slowly will cause the coat hanger to revolve in the same direction.

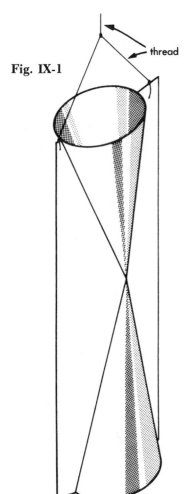

Fig. IX-1

thread

IX. *Conical Hourglass Generator*

Patterns, pages 79-81

Assembly Instructions

1. Cut out Figures IX-A and IX-B, forming Cones IX-A and IX-B. Crease forward slightly along broken lines and tape or glue tabs to form two separate cones.
2. Cut out Figures IX-C and IX-D, forming the two baffles. Crease along broken lines to make a right angle. Tape or glue Baffle Tabs to sides of one cone. Baffle IX-C will be on the right side, Baffle IX-D on the left.
3. Invert the second cone and tape or glue the Baffle Tabs to its sides. The design of the baffles creates a tilted angle. Tie thread to each baffle and suspend as shown in Figure IX-1, so the device can rotate at an angle, approximately one foot above eye level.

It will rotate when stared at.

X. *Twisted Hourglass Generator*

Patterns, pages 83-89

This generator (invented by Woodrow W. Ward of Houston, Texas, in 1970) represents the first American breakthrough in the psionic field. Mr. Ward's flair for empirical advances into futuristic technologies has resulted in many similar devices designed to control and manipulate pyramidal and biological energies.

Assembly Instructions

1. Cut out Figures X-A through X-D and fold to form two pyramids. Use tape or glue to seal the bottoms and sides.
2. Cut out the four baffles, Figures X-E through X-H. Bend baffles slightly on dotted lines according to instructions. Tape or glue the two baffles, Figures X-E and X-F, to the two left-hand corners of one pyramid (see Figure X-2).
3. Tape the two remaining baffles, Figures X-G and X-H, to the two right-hand corners of the same pyramid (see Figure X-3).
4. Invert the second pyramid, and tape or glue one of the four baffle edges to each of its four corners as illustrated in Figure X-4.

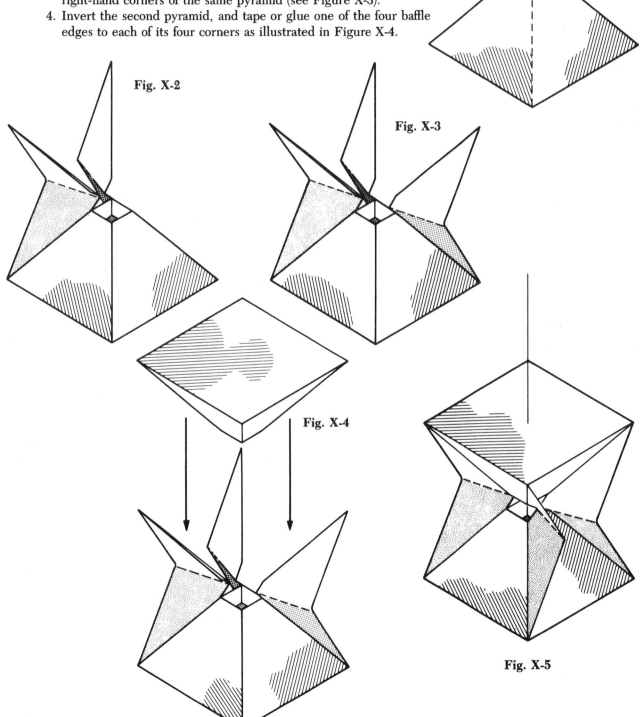

Fig. X-1

Fig. X-2

Fig. X-3

Fig. X-4

Fig. X-5

Since the two sets of baffles are not uniform, the top pyramid will be slightly tilted, and its four corners will not line up evenly with the four corners of the bottom pyramid. The generator should resemble a tilted, twisted hourglass. You can bend and twist the top pyramid slightly to create the effect illustrated in Figure X-5.

Once it is completed, attach a two-foot length of thread to the base of the top pyramid slightly off center to assist the device in revolving in a "warped" or twisted rotation pattern. The thread can be attached with a piece of tape; or before taping the base to the top pyramid, push a sewing needle and thread through the base from the inside. Tie a heavy knot so the thread will not pass through, then tape the base to the pyramid.

Suspend the apparatus at about eye level. Be certain the area is free from small air currents. When it comes to rest, concentrate your gaze upon the baffles or the opening in the center. In about a minute or two it should begin to move and rotate slowly.

Stand approximately ten feet away at first, then try various distances for effects. Your gaze must remain fixed upon the generator, but there is no need for deep concentration. A steady gaze will produce about five or six rpm's. Glancing away quickly, then returning your gaze to the structure seems to activate it more quickly, and moving your gaze from side to side tends to produce greater revolutions.

XI. *Dowsing Rod*

Radiesthesia—or dowsing—has been practiced for thousands of years throughout the world to locate underground streams, ore deposits, mines, tunnels, metal objects, and so forth. Most dowsers use a forked twig cut from a peach, willow, or shade tree. Holding a forked end in each hand and walking slowly across the land with the rod parallel to the earth, dowsers find that the rod dips or bends when passing over anomalies deep in the earth. It was first thought that only a few people possessed the ability to dowse successfully, but recent tests have now revealed that almost everyone is endowed with the sensitivity necessary to cause metal dowsing.

Tests reveal that dowsing rods are also sensitive to electrostatic and electromagnetic fields in the human body. Investigators have not discovered why or how dowsing works, but they agree that the human body's sensitivity is registered by the actions of the rod or forked twig, and that the human body is a vital part of the dowsing instrument.

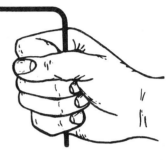

28 inches   6 inches

Fig. XI-1

Fig. XI-2

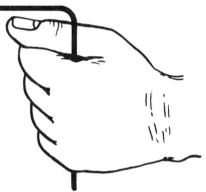

Metal dowsing rods can be fashioned quite easily from two wire coat hangers, although copper and aluminum wire seem to be a little more responsive. Unbend the coat hangers and straighten the wire into a straight piece thirty-four inches long. Bend the last six inches of each rod at a right angle to act as a "handle" as shown in Figure XI-1.

Hold the two rods loosely, one in each hand, about twelve inches apart with the "grips" vertical in your hands and the large "pointers" parallel to the ground. When you walk over an underground pipe or similar anomaly, the rods will cross over each other. (However, if your blood is Rh negative, they will usually angle outward to either side.) The rods will react similarly when passed over the apex of a precise pyramid shape.

You can test the accuracy of these simple dowsing rods by locating underground gas and water pipes which run the length of alleyways. Smaller but similar pipes are buried beneath the ground in most backyards. In rural areas, the rods will be activated by underground streams, wells, metal objects—in short, whatever object the dowser is concentrating on at the time. Rods will even react to spare change hidden under the corner of a rug, and will cross when the experimenter names the coin—penny, nickel, dime, or quarter —correctly.

Radiesthesia rods can be easily constructed in such a way that they act as an aurameter—detecting energy waves which emanate from the human body. For centuries, psychics have claimed to be able to see this radiance and called it the human "aura." In the photographic process invented by Semyon Davidovich Kirlian and his wife Valentina, this energy resembles the aurora borealis or miniature bolts of flashing lightning and pulsating multicolored sparks and flares.

Since individuals generate different energy patterns, many personalities "clash" for no apparent reason, while other individuals seem to be completely compatible with each other. Initial tests indicate that aurameters are capable of identifying individuals who are harmonious with each other. This does not necessarily mean that all these individuals would reflect similar likes and dislikes or demonstrate a stereotype pattern. A group of compatible persons could be made up of individuals from all walks of life who seem totally dissimilar by all outward appearances. However, working as a team, they would perform remarkably well.

An aurameter is a simple device requiring little technical skill to construct. Materials usually found in the home or at your local department store are all that are required:

* A six-foot length of bare copper or aluminum wire approximately $1/16$ inch thick. The wire must be solid, not stranded.
* A wooden or plastic handle at least four inches in length.
* A small metal weight such as a fishing sinker. The lead fishing sinker with a hole through the center works fine; so does the type with one side open since this can be crimped closed with a pair of pliers.

Assembly Instructions

1. Using six feet of solid, bare copper or aluminum wire, coil or wrap one end around the handle seven revolutions (see Figure XII-1). The handle should be at least four inches in length and its coils approximately one to one-and-a-half inches in diameter. On the last revolution, bend the wire at a right angle so that it travels parallel to the handle as illustrated in Figure XII-1.
2. Use a cylindrical object such as a drinking glass or length of pipe to form three loops in the remaining wire (see Figure XII-2). The cylinder should be between two-and-a-half and three inches in diameter. Now remove the cylinder and bend the wire at a right angle at the top of the last loop, as shown in Figure XII-3.

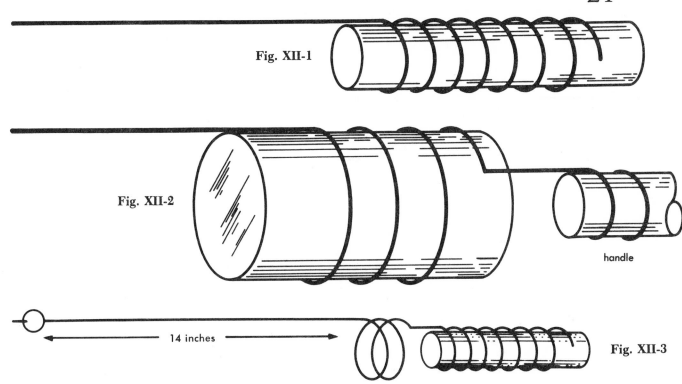

Fig. XII-1

Fig. XII-2

handle

14 inches

Fig. XII-3

3. Attach a metal weight approximately fourteen inches from the last loop (see Figure XII-3). Snip off any wire which extends beyond the weight. (Usually a few inches of wire is left over, depending on the diameter of the cylinder used to form the loops.) A fishing sinker with a hole through the center works fine.

One need not hold critical dimensions when forming the aurameter, but the finished product should be very flexible and sensitive to the slightest movement. If it isn't, extend the loops slightly by merely pulling forward about half an inch.

Here's how it works:

Grasp the handle in either hand and hold the weight at the end of the wire over the head of the person being tested. The weight will revolve clockwise, counterclockwise, or in a vertical or horizontal pattern. Next, hold the weight over each individually extended finger of the subject's hand. Again, when picking up the aura energies from each finger, it will react in one of the four patterns. For example, the index finger may demonstrate a clockwise rotation, while the ring finger may manifest horizontal configurations.

Individuals can be classified as either horizontal, vertical, clockwise, or counterclockwise, according to the most prominent configurations which occur when the aurameter is held over various areas of the body. The head, palms of the hands, fingers, solar plexus, and feet

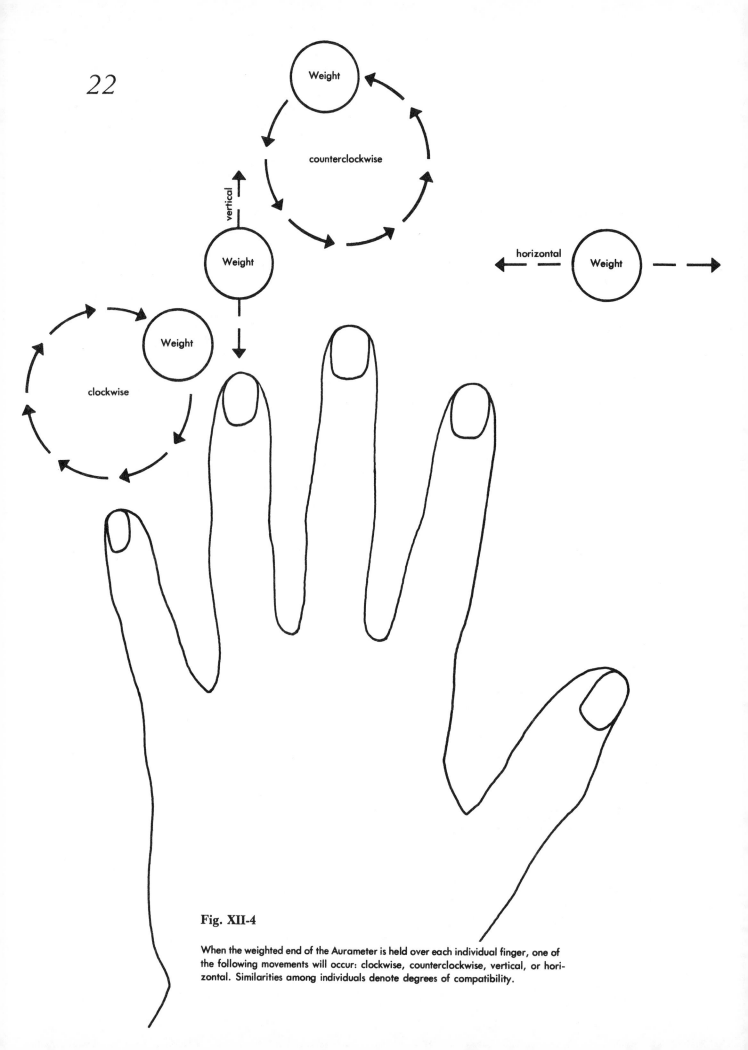

Fig. XII-4

When the weighted end of the Aurameter is held over each individual finger, one of the following movements will occur: clockwise, counterclockwise, vertical, or horizontal. Similarities among individuals denote degrees of compatibility.

create different patterns, and since thousands of persons must be tested in order to complete an accurate compatibility chart, additional research will be required before 100% accuracy in personality judgment is achieved. Slight pattern variances do not represent total incompatibility among individuals, but if you prove to be 90% clockwise or horizontal, you can rest assured that it would be difficult for you to work efficiently with a person whose patterns reflected extreme vertical movements.

The aurameter is also capable of detecting the energy emanating from the pyramid structure. When held at the apex, the weight travels in various configurations. When one side of the pyramid is removed and the weight is placed within the interior, horizontal patterns occur—except at the one-third level where the weight circles in a clockwise movement, indicating that the pyramid shape creates a vortex of energy traveling in a clockwise motion. A yes-or-no answering game can be played by using both the pyramid and the aurameter. Hold the weighted end over the apex of the pyramid and ask a question aloud which requires an affirmative or a negative answer. A vertical movement signifies yes; horizontal suggests no.

It is difficult to pass judgment on the game's accuracy, especially since the energy accumulated in the pyramid shape is enigmatic and unharnessed. But certainly the answers received are often surprising and could be developed to a higher degree of reliability by the experimenter who's willing to practice. Essentially, this is a means of "dowsing" for information, receiving answers directly from the subconscious, and has untold applications beyond mere fortune-telling.

_____ *Patterns*

The special heavy paper in this section has been selected for the greatest ease in assembly, as well as for the most effective psionic performance. No tracing or extra reinforcing is necessary.

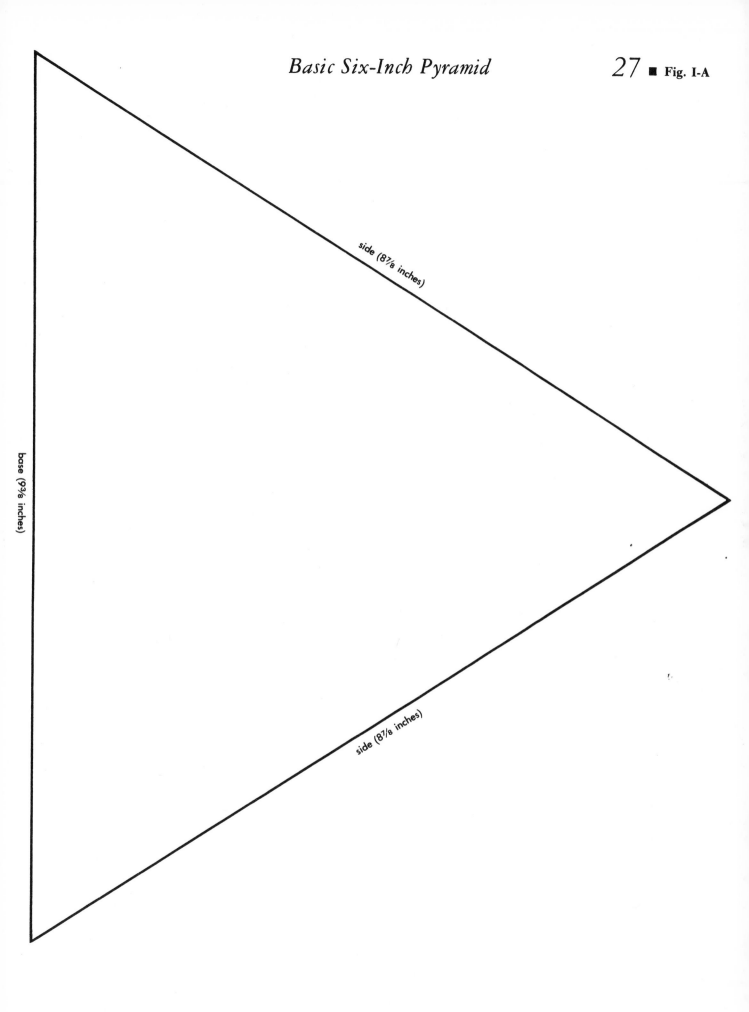

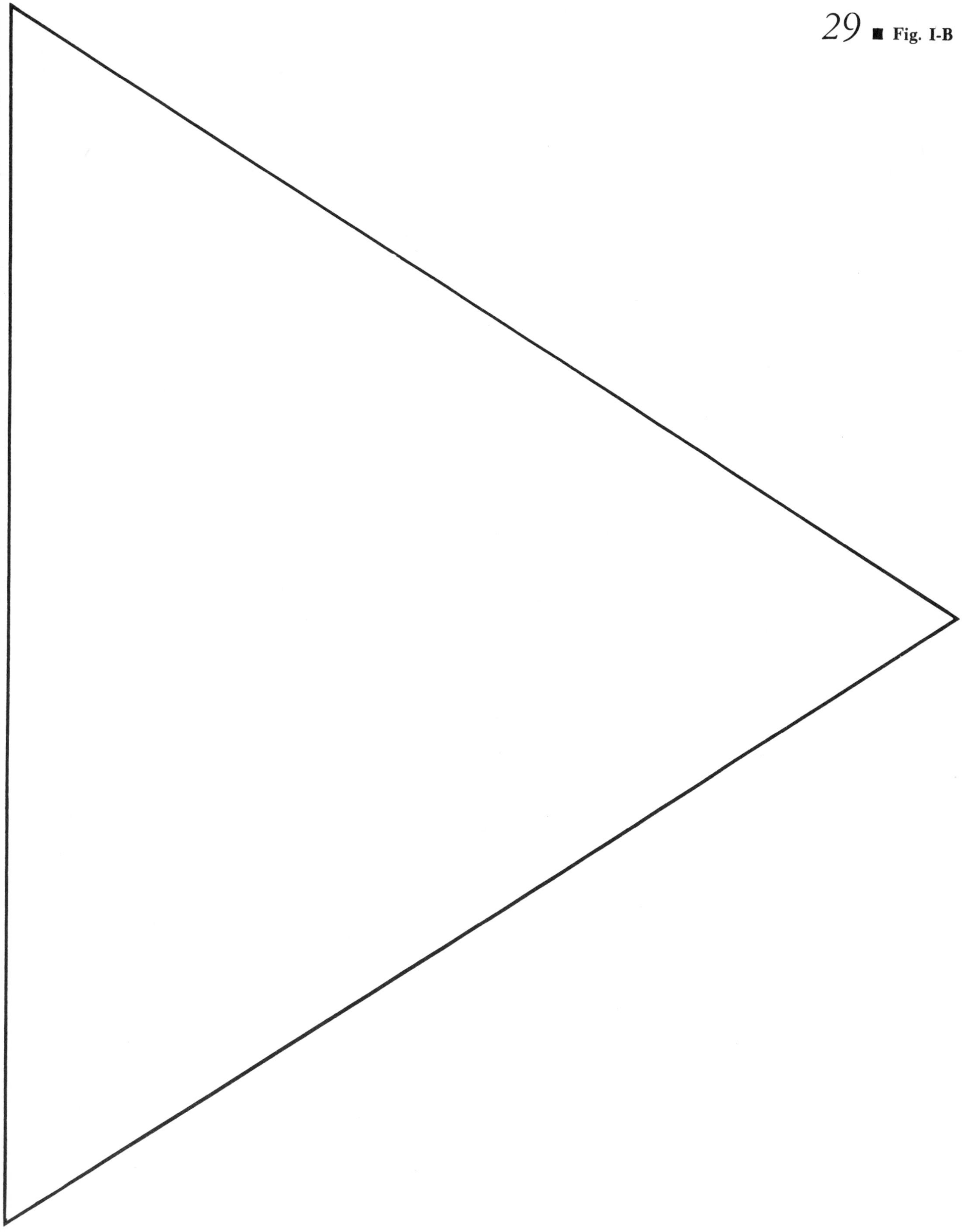

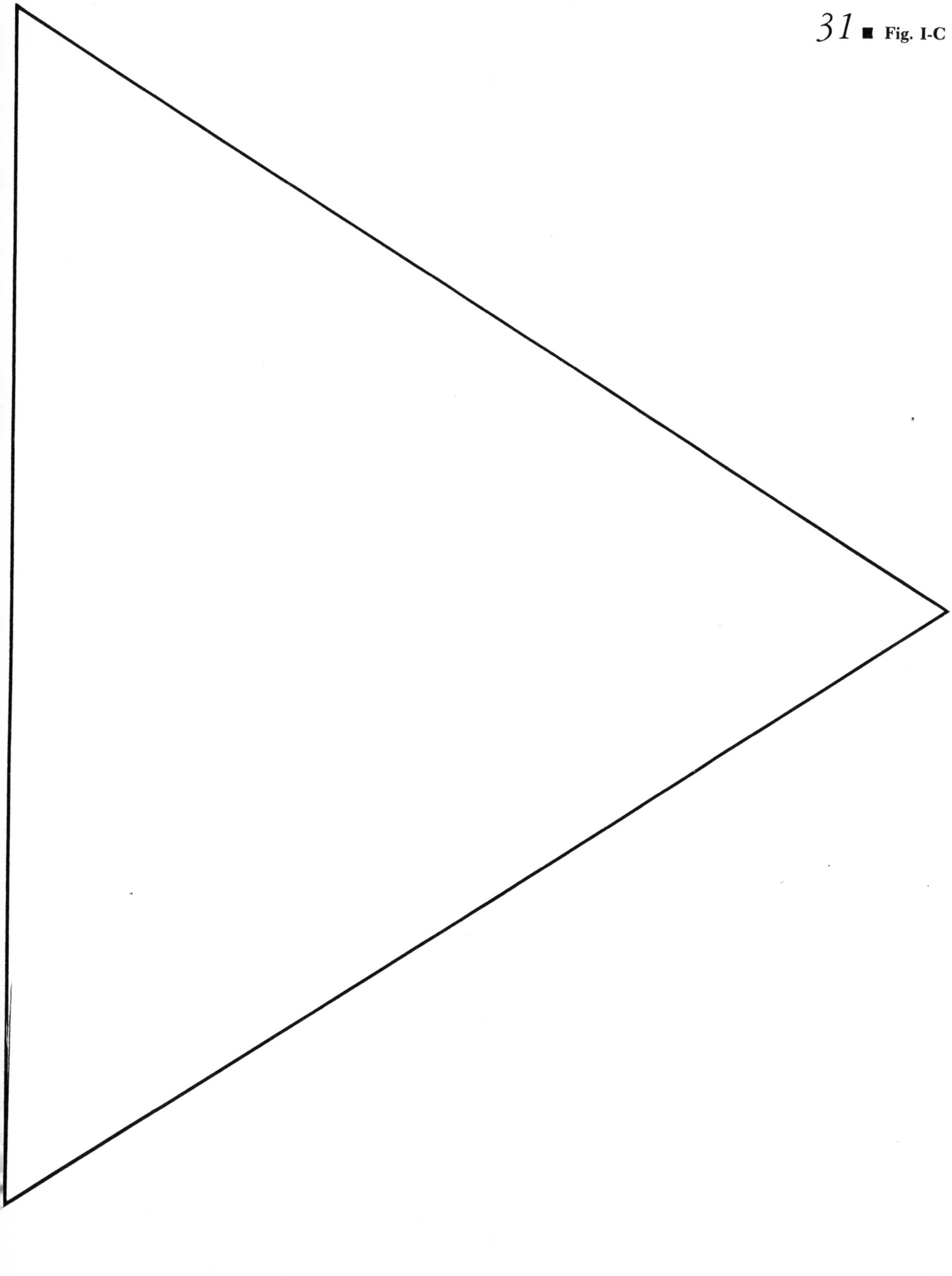

base

crease on dotted line

Tab A

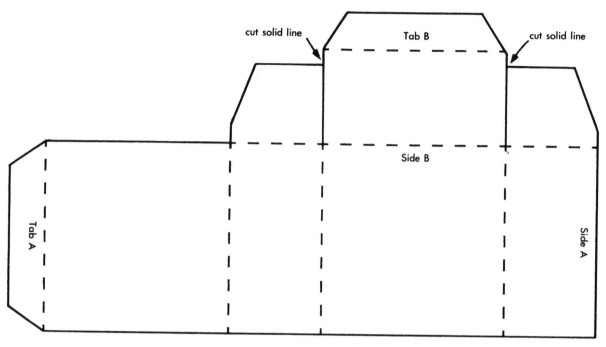

Cut out the above pattern along solid lines and crease forward on all dotted lines. Glue or tape Tab A inside Side A. Fold Tab B and place inside Side B.

The square can be cut out and placed atop the two-inch platform to support objects larger than a razor blade. The slight increase in height does not affect experiments.

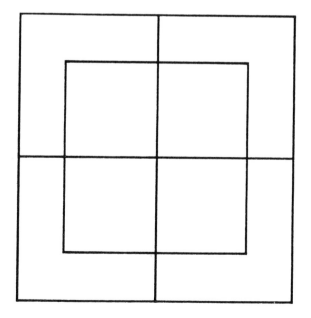

NOTE: You may want to line the back of this and the next three pages with crinkled aluminum foil *before* cutting. Cut out all circles marked X.

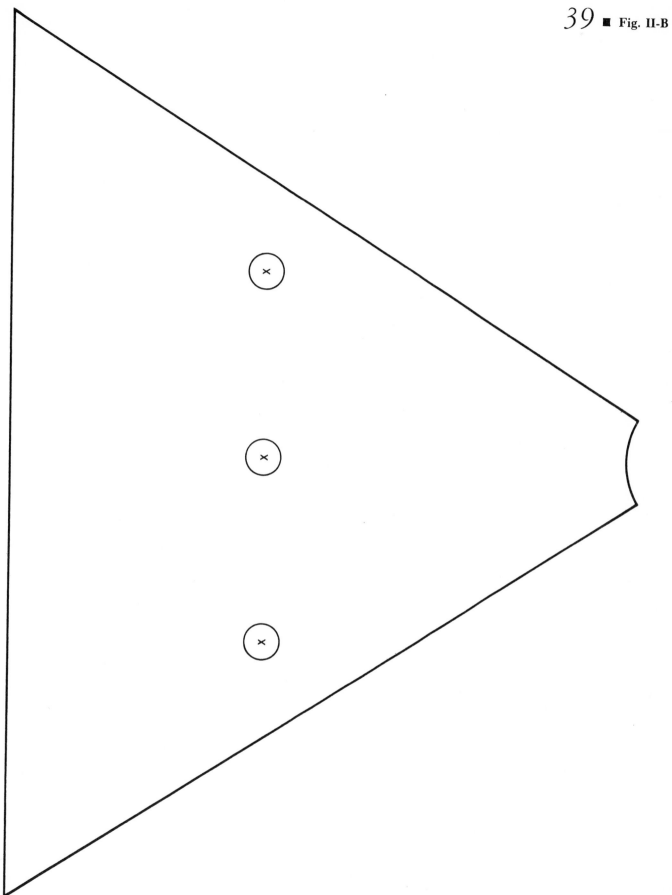

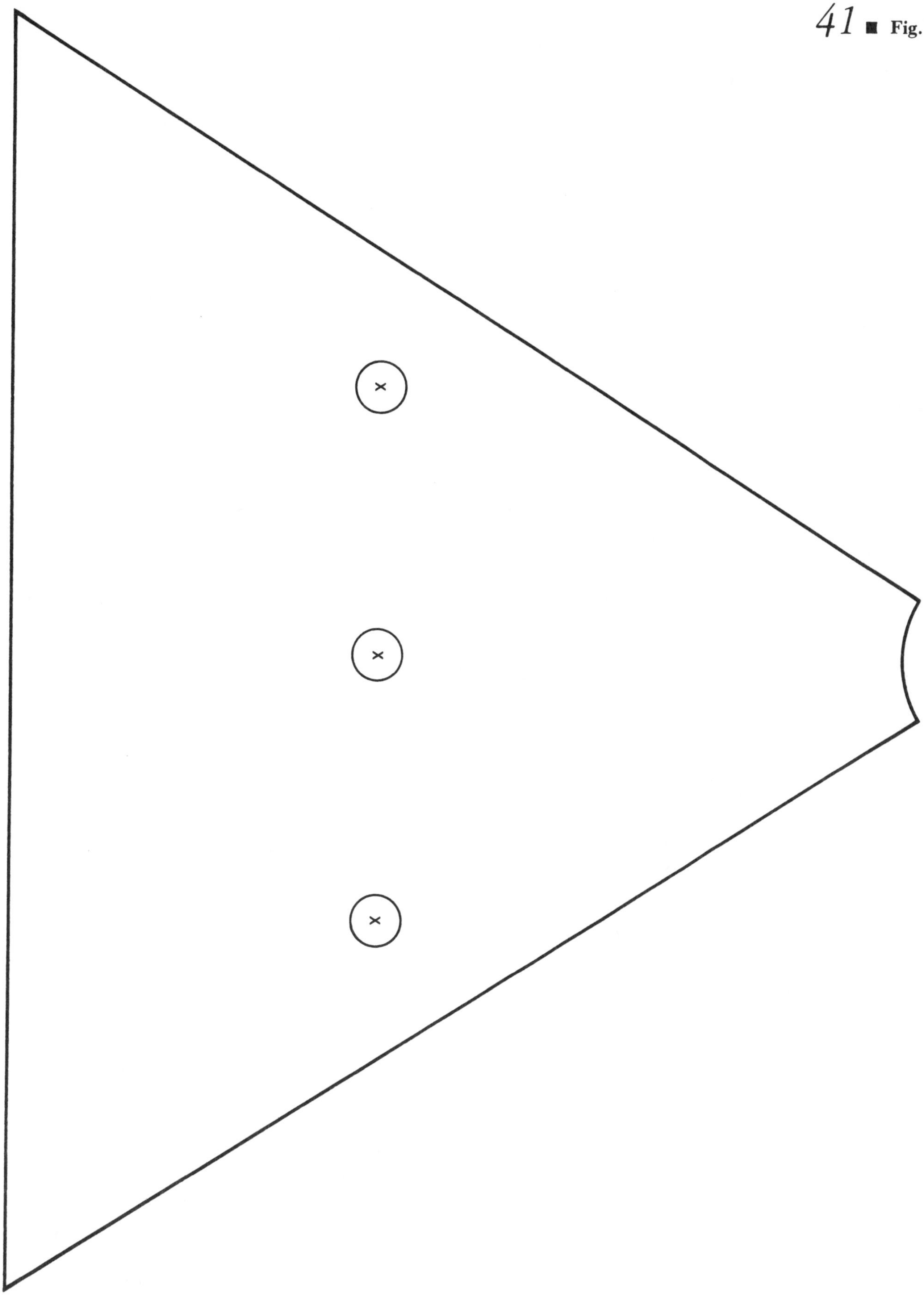

crease along dotted line

tab

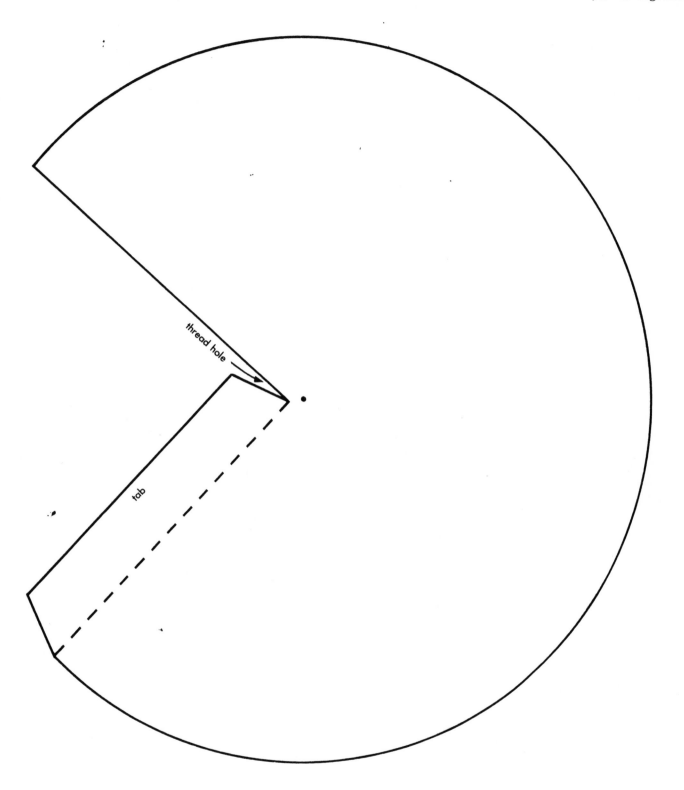

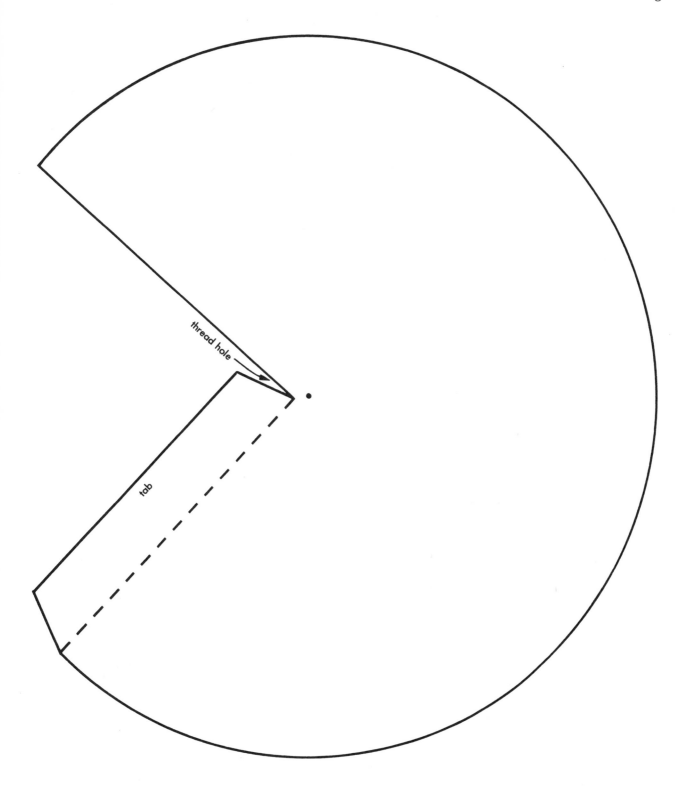

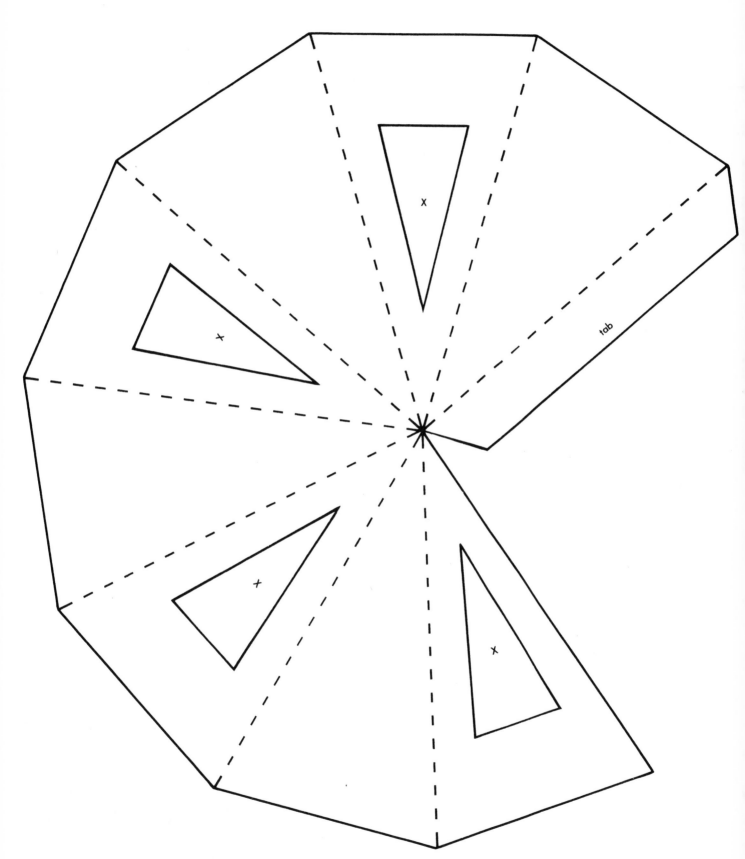

tab

Cut out along solid lines. Crease slightly along broken lines. Cut out the four triangular openings marked X. Glue or tape tab to inside of opposite triangle to form pyramidal structure.

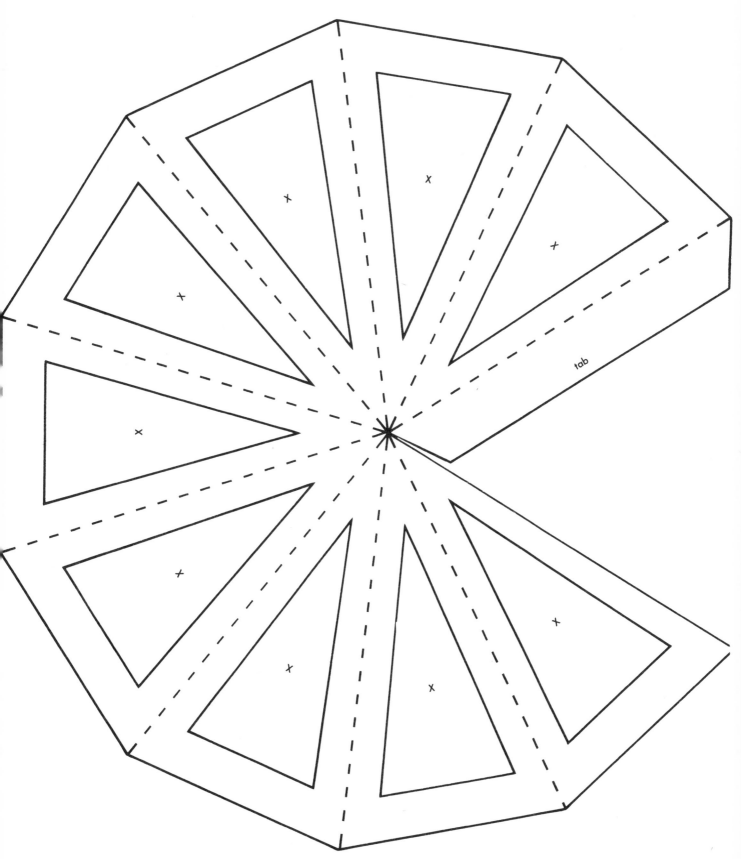

tab

Cut out along solid lines. Crease forward slightly along broken lines. Cut out all central triangles marked X. Glue or tape tab in place to form structure.

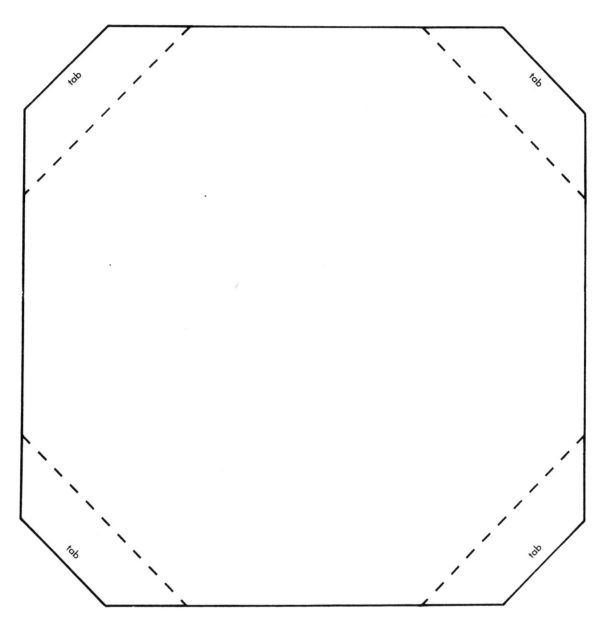

Cut along solid lines. Fold tabs inward along broken lines, and glue or tape tabs just inside bottom of Pyramidal Structure IV-A. Remember to run needle and thread up through the apex of Structure IV-A *before* gluing base in place.

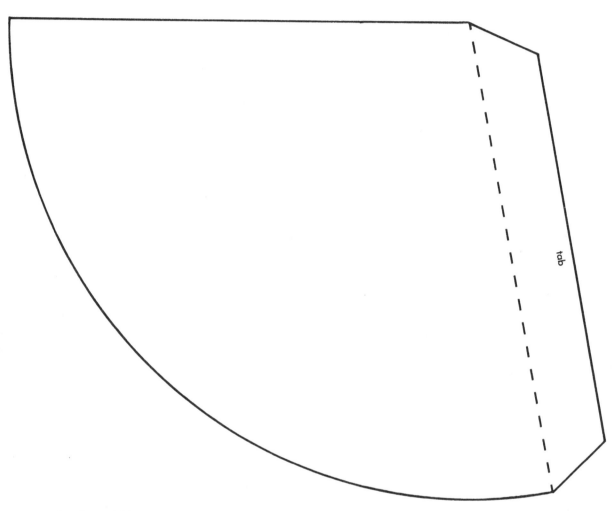

tab

Cut along solid lines; crease along broken line. Tape or glue tab inside opposite edge to form cone.

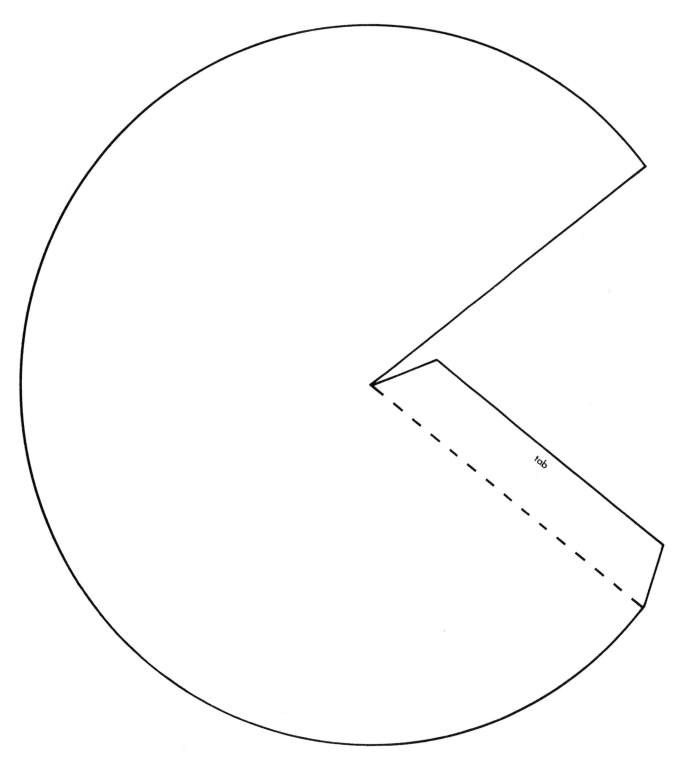

tab

Cut along solid lines; crease along broken line. Tape or glue tab inside to form the base cone of the generator.

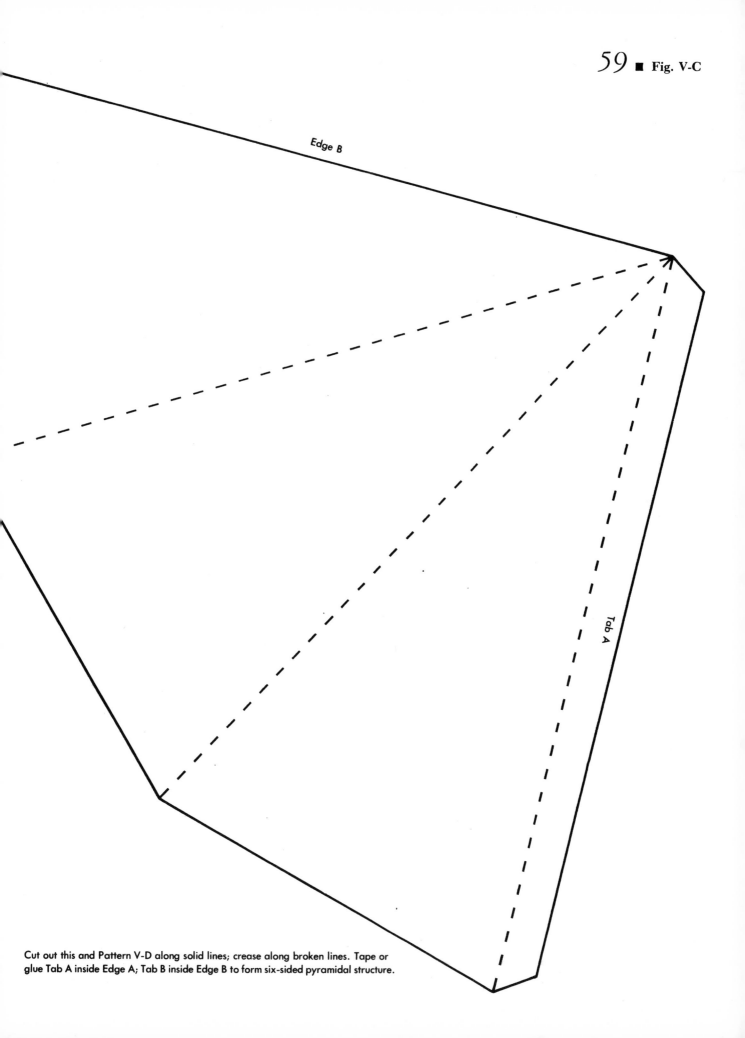

Edge B

Tab A

Cut out this and Pattern V-D along solid lines; crease along broken lines. Tape or glue Tab A inside Edge A; Tab B inside Edge B to form six-sided pyramidal structure.

Edge A

Tab B

Cut out along solid lines; crease along broken lines.

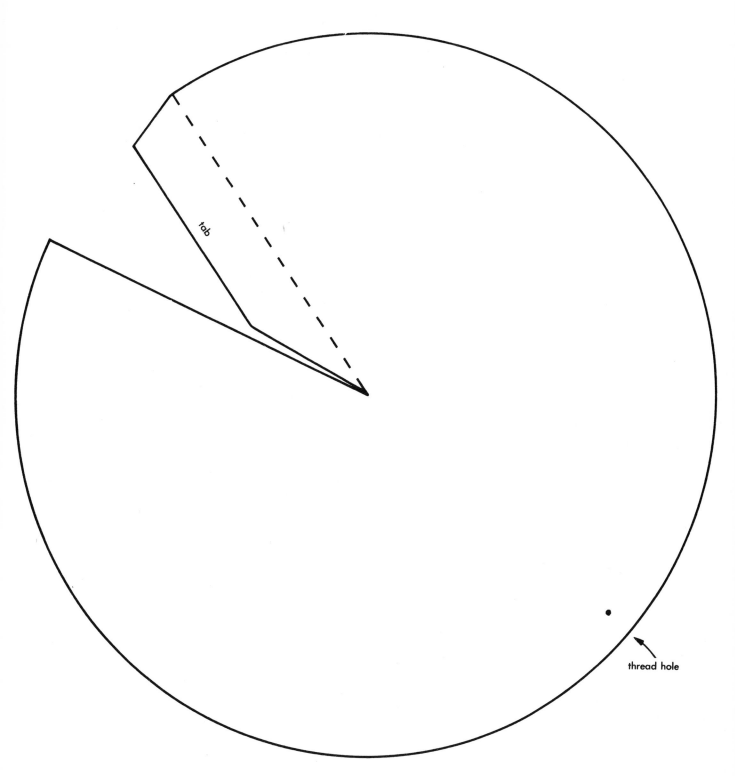

tab

thread hole

Cut out, then glue or tape tab to form cone.

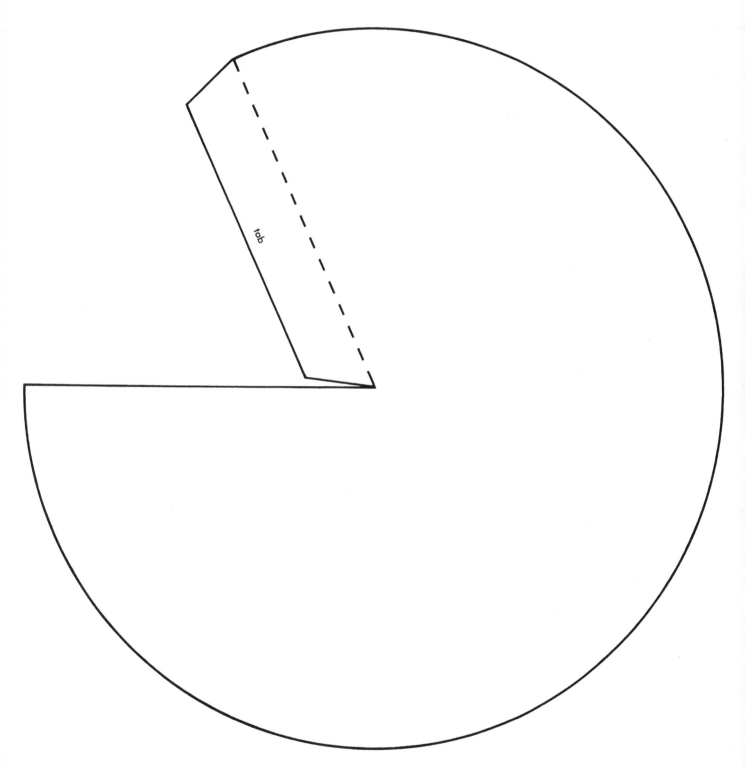

tab

Assemble and glue to inside of Cone VI-A.

■ **Fig. VI-C**
■ **Fig. VI-D**

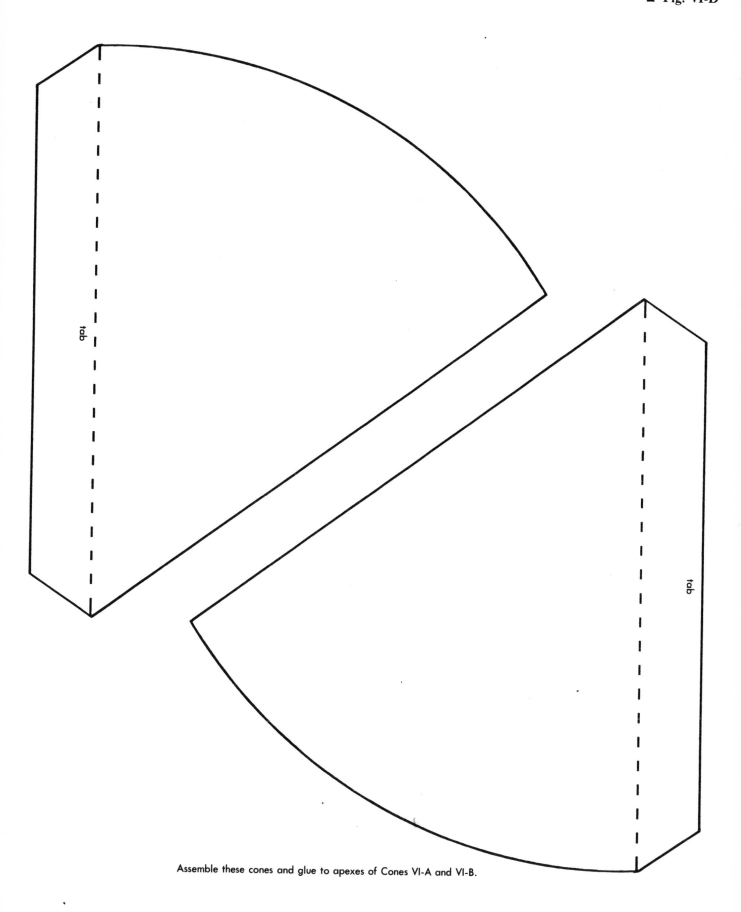

tab

tab

Assemble these cones and glue to apexes of Cones VI-A and VI-B.

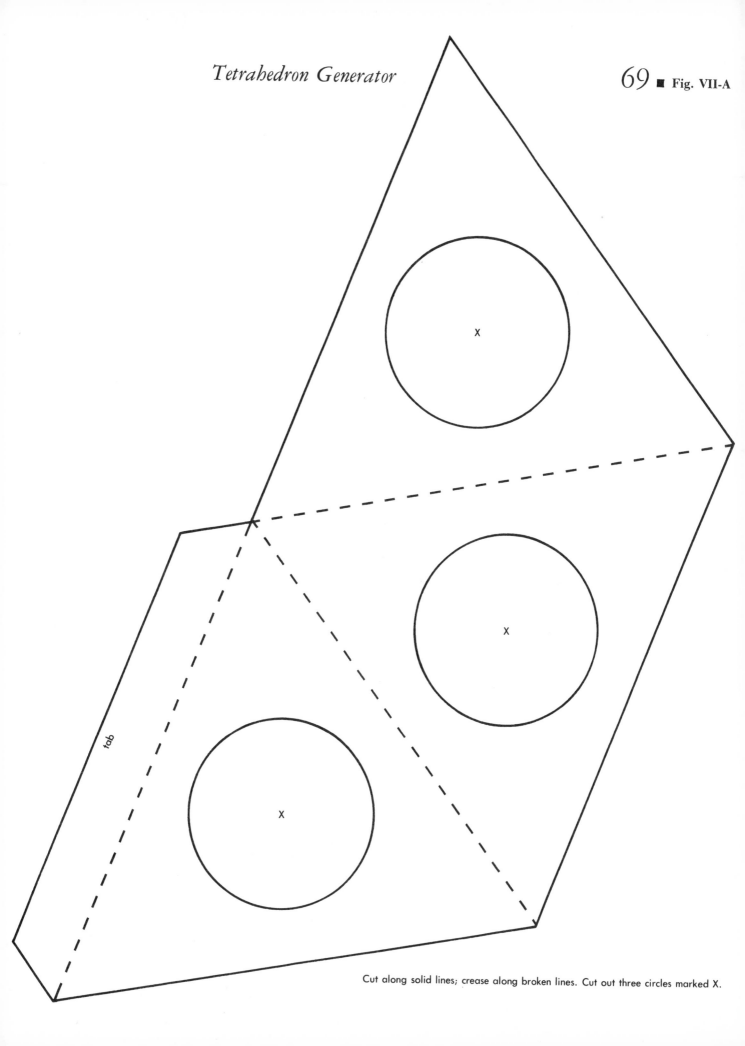

Tetrahedron Generator

tab

Cut along solid lines; crease along broken lines. Cut out three circles marked X.

■ Fig. VII-B
■ Fig. VII-C

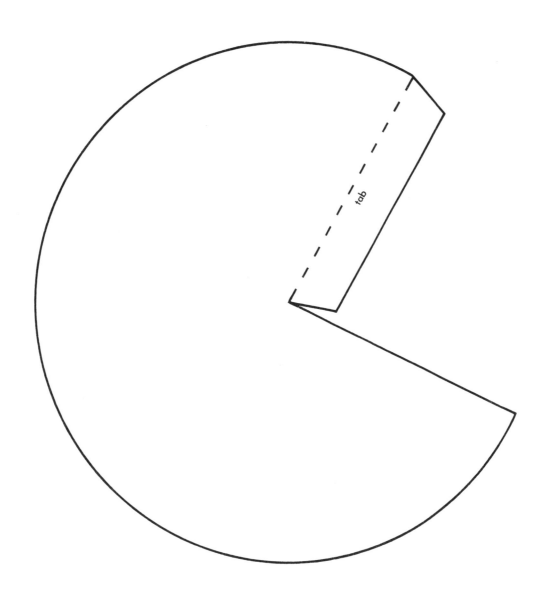

tab

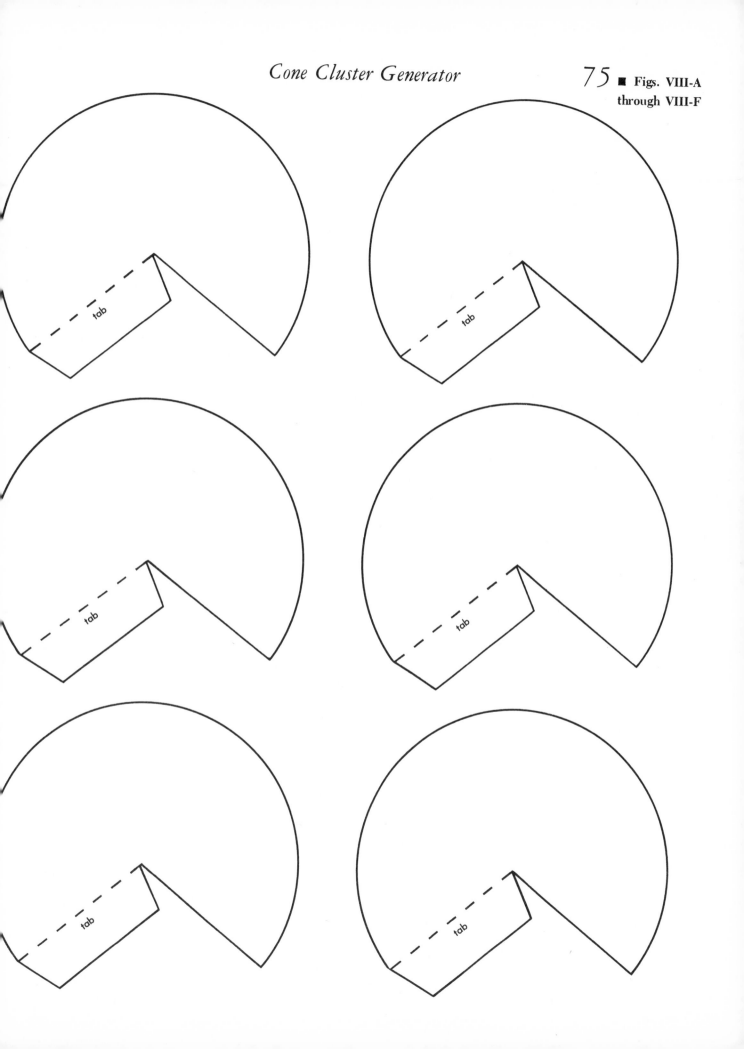

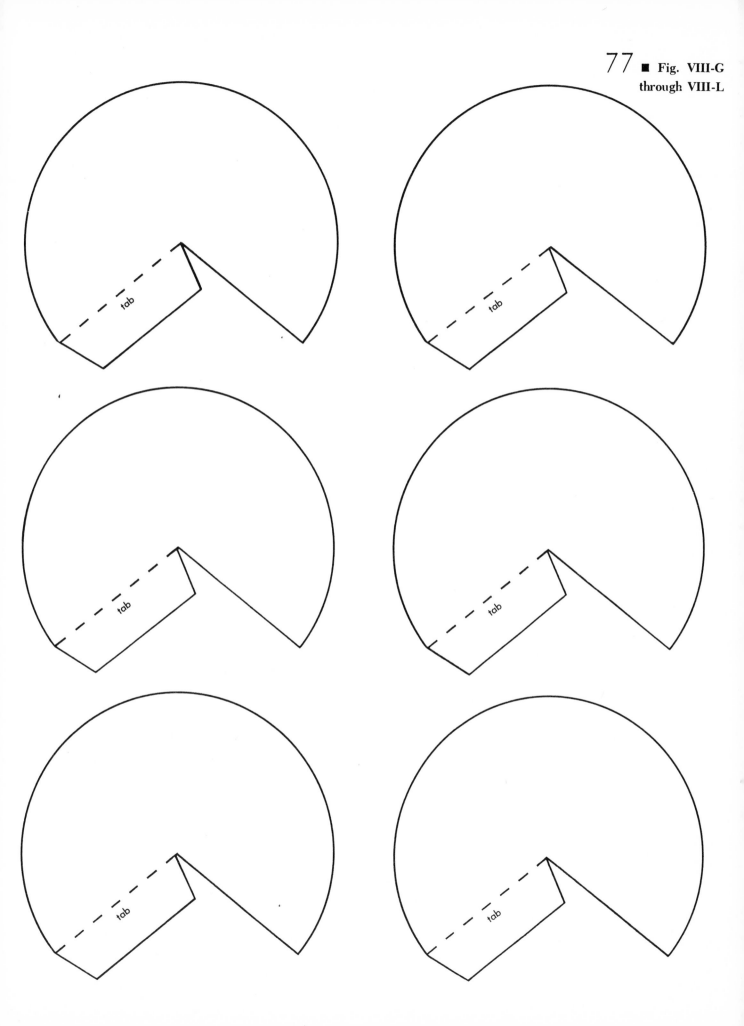

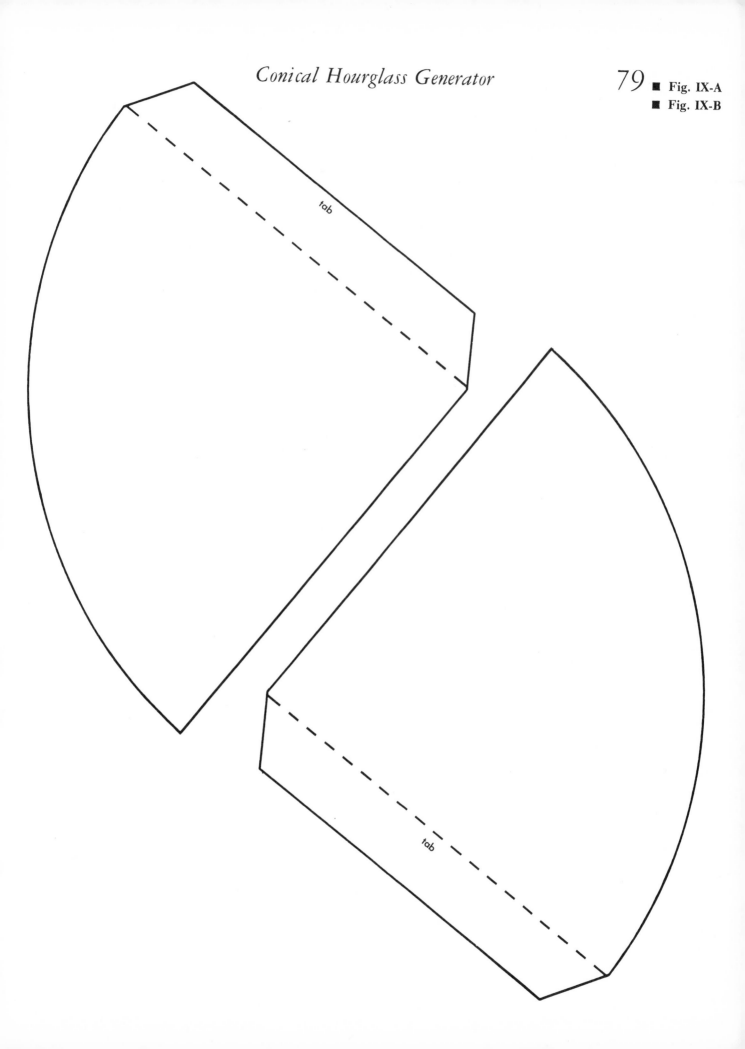

tab

tab

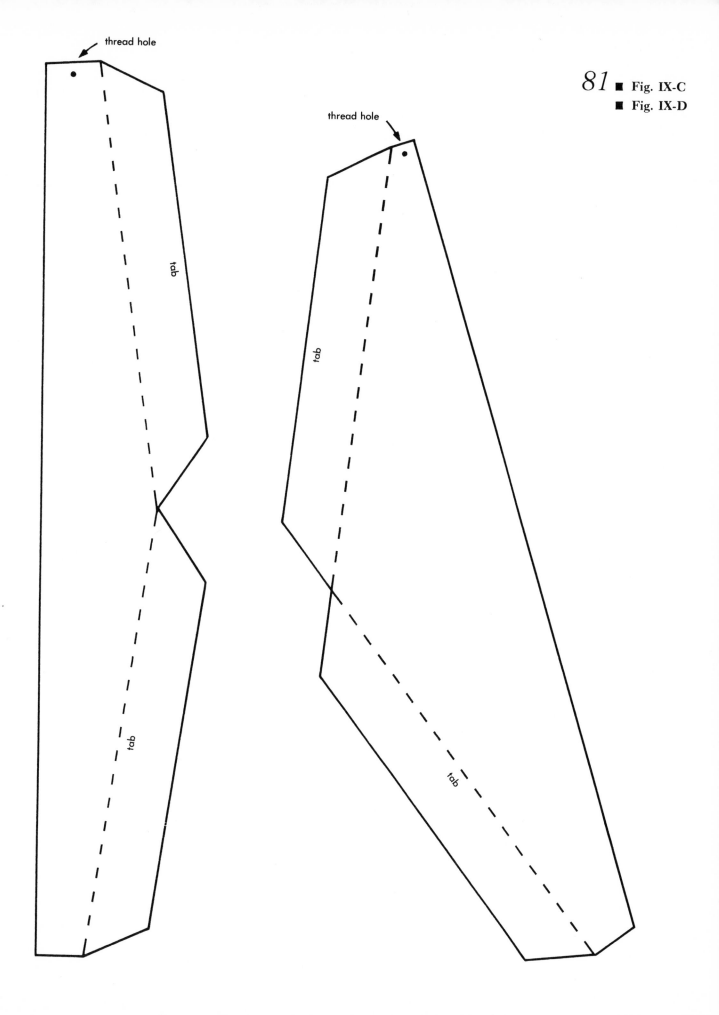

thread hole

tab

tab

thread hole

tab

tab

81 ■ Fig. IX-C
■ Fig. IX-D

tab

tab

tab

Cut out this and the following pattern along solid lines; crease along broken lines. Fold and tape or glue tabs inside opposite edges to form two pyramids.

tab

tab

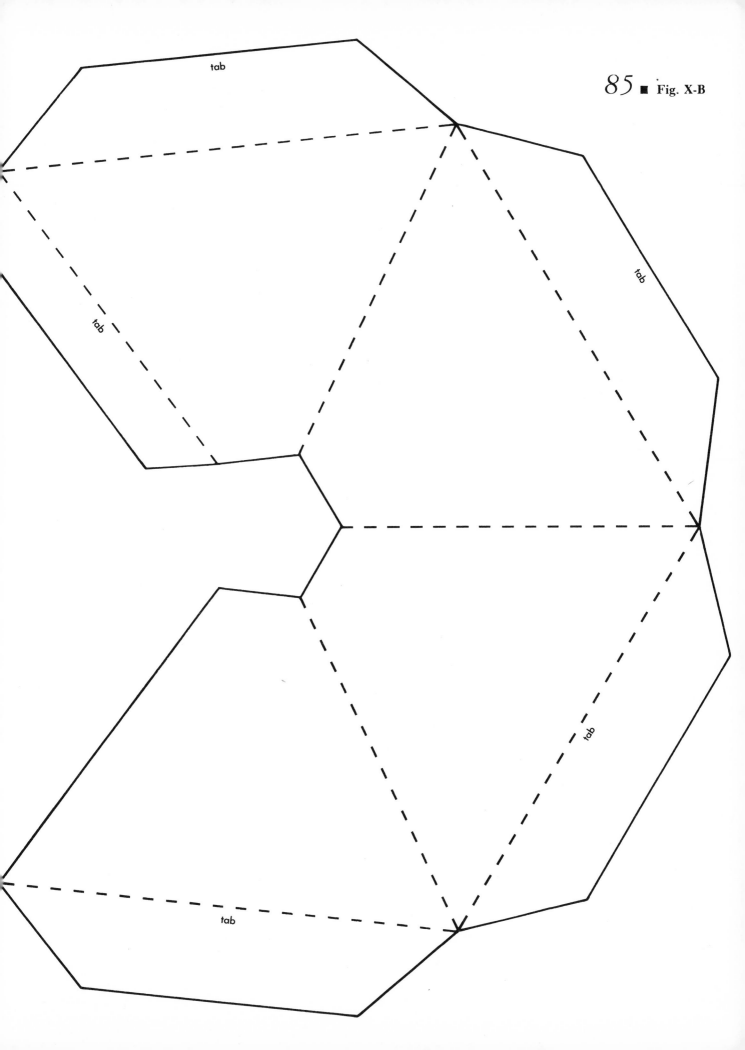

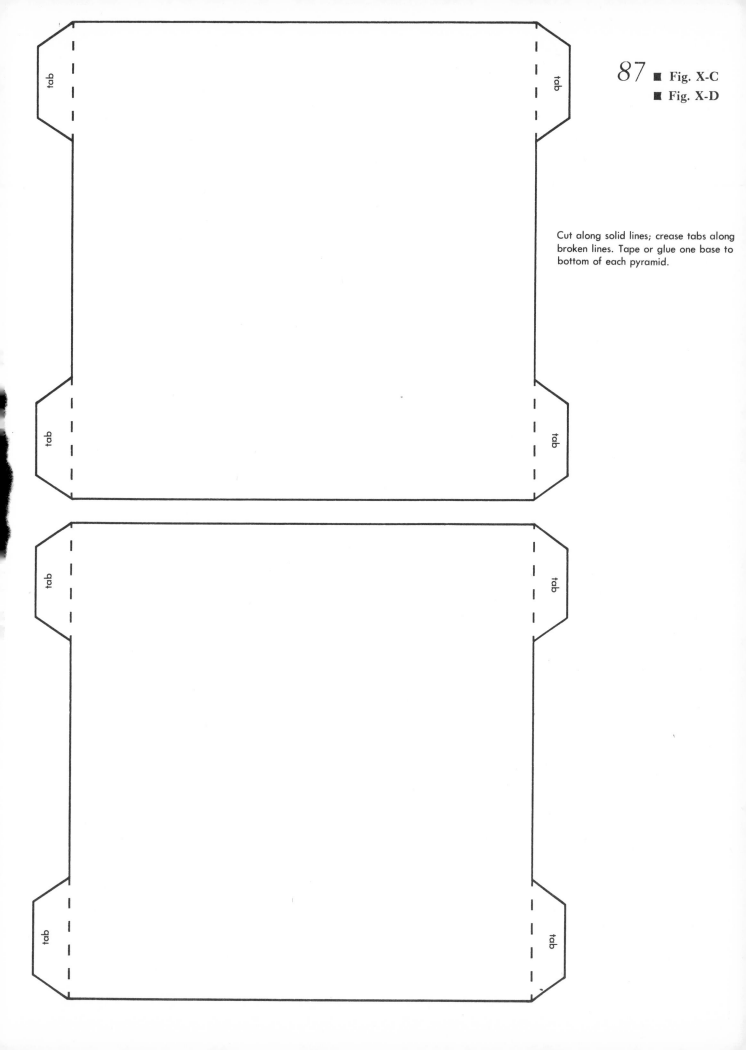

87 ■ **Fig. X-C**
■ **Fig. X-D**

Cut along solid lines; crease tabs along broken lines. Tape or glue one base to bottom of each pyramid.

tab
tab
tab
tab
tab
tab
tab
tab

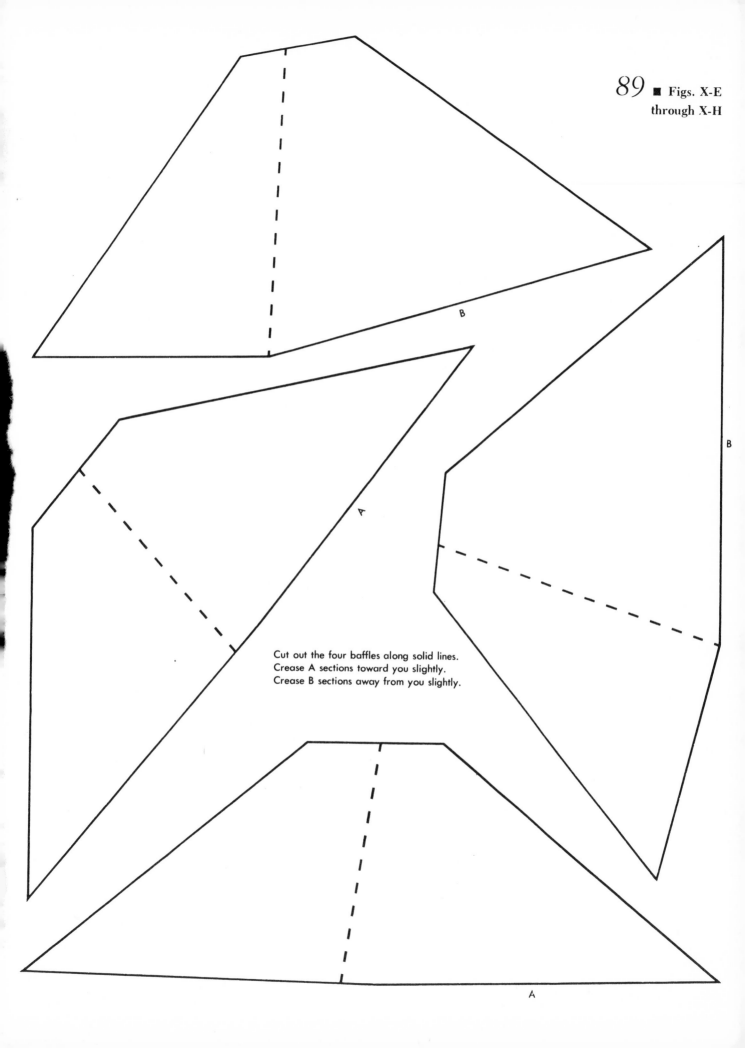

B

B

A

Cut out the four baffles along solid lines.
Crease A sections toward you slightly.
Crease B sections away from you slightly.

A